SALES

SYSTEMS

SALES TACTICS FOR BUSINESS GROWTH
SKILLS TO SELL IDEAS, PRODUCTS AND SERVICES

KWABENA OBENG DARKO

SALES SYSTEMS

© Kwabena Obeng Darko

March, 2024

E-mail your questions and comments to the author at:

info@obengdarko.com.gh

www.obengdarko.com.gh

Designed and Printed and Published by:

Odtrah

P . O . BOX MS 13

Mile 7-Achimota

Accra-Ghana

TEL: +233 24 6631874

SALES SYSTEMS

SALES TACTICS FOR BUSINESS GROWTH
SKILLS TO SELL IDEAS, PRODUCTS AND SERVICES

KWABENA OBENG DARKO

DEDICATION

This book is dedicated to African market women.

AUTHOR'S NOTES AND ACKNOWLEDGMENT

To my wife, Marie and children, Yaa, Awuraa and Kwabena, love you as always. You are all a blessing.

CONTENTS

INTRODUCTION

If you want to find where they make money, go to where they sell services or products. Those who sell profit from what they sell because they exchange what they sell for cash. You will always see products exchanged for money when you go to any market. Whatever products will have to be sold to the people who need them? It isn't easy to build any business that cannot sell what they produce, service, or product. It is basic arithmetic to know that if you want where money is made easily every day, you go to the market. The market women are not poor. They sell every day. Don't pity the Provision shop owner; she sees money every day. Those who don't understand money don't understand sales, and those who don't understand sales don't understand money. Selling is money, and that is primary financial education. The economy we have is mainly built on selling the things people need. Whatever we produce in our economy must be sold, or there is no business.

We must learn to sell and sell intentionally. Sales is one of the best wealth creation structures, and when understood early, it can help anybody succeed financially and easily. Many people have become rich not because they are intelligent per se but because they only happen to sell products or services that are in high demand.

- Selling demands that you sell what is in need.

- You sell what is in demand.

- You sell what people are looking for.

Many don't have credit cards or loans to buy cars or house mortgages. Our credit card is selling. It is very easy to start, and we can start with as little as we have. Many people underestimate the volume of transactions and the amount of money generated in the many retail shops across our country. That is where the money is. We must learn how to sell and know that if you want to start a business, look at selling. A large part of our sales economy is in retail, from selling construction materials and tools to agriculture tools and products to fashion, education, health, etc.

- Learn to sell intentionally.

- Selling is a financial freedom tool.

- The success of your business is on sales.

- Those who know how to sell are the ones making the money.

We must develop our own sales processes and protocols. Systems are required for success and continuity in any sphere. Success in sales also requires systems. Sales systems would have to include our sales targets, sales skills, sales team, sales culture, customers and product knowledge, and ability to use technology, especially social media, to sell our products. Proper sales systems are designed for us to meet our sales goals and to handle the nos and the objections that come from customers. Our sales experience must be based on our culture and the uniqueness of our environment.

Not many know that selling is a skill developed with knowledge, training, and practice over time. Selling depends not on the buying but on the skills of the one selling. Offer great sales experience that your customers will always love to have. Serve your customers with much respect and decorum. Those you sell to should feel welcome and comfortable. Many times, we go to buy products from shops, and it is almost always like we are begging them to buy from them. It is nearly as if they are doing us a favor. This kind of attitude comes from non-intentional sales culture and training.

This book discusses the systems we need to implement to improve our sales and grow our businesses.

CHAPTER 1

SALES

S elling is cash to the business and must be done well. Go the extra mile always to make sales, and your business will continue to grow. You don't have to have perfect products to make sales; you have to know how to sell to those who buy from you, the value, and the sales intentionality. We want to see our sales culture in our country and continent improve. Many of our businesses lose lots of sales because we are not improving our sales training and systems.

These systems must be built on the culture and the traditions that we have. We just have to improve our businesses by improving our sales systems. We don't have to supplant what we have with the so-called international sales techniques. Africa must improve what we and we must improve our sales systems to sell our products and services for the growth of our businesses.

- Train yourself as a business owner and train your team.
- Train with our culture in mind.

How do we handle the issues that come up after sales are handled professionally if we are informed in sales? Our telephone and online sales skills all come from the sales training that we give to our sales team. Selling is cash and selling is a skill. Our businesses do well when we know how to sell our products and services.

Develop a sales culture in your business that drives sales no matter the conditions and that can be achieved through structures designed to train the sales team to achieve continually increasing sales. You need a sales team that is grateful for the work that they do and is truthful in their work. Selling is not superstitious and is not religious. This is the case many of our people would want to bring their religious practices and beliefs to sell their products and services. You have to intentionally work on this in yourself and your sales culture and business. Selling is a system that is built on purpose. You have to bring home this basic understanding that selling is the systems and emotions of the people involved. There are different customers that we sell to with different buying power, different beliefs, and different levels of education. Some techniques are developed to improve sales.

- Make sure your buyers are comfortable.

- The pricing is right for our customer category.

- Understanding the culture that we sell in.

- Right product knowledge

- The sales team working together

- Knowing what to say when the customer does not want to buy.

- Selling is about emotions and how well we can handle customers and their emotions have a direct effect on our sales results.

- Smell good and look good. People love nice smells and nice things.

- We must have sales targets that we have to meet on a daily, weekly, monthly, and yearly basis.

We should understand that we are not there to demand respect from our customers. What we have to do is to serve them and sell to them. Speak the language of your customers and speak at the level that they understand. That is the point they appreciate your service. Sales dynamics change on special occasions and holidays like Easter or Christmas or any time there is a big event. These should be kept in mind. Train your team not to bed customers for money and must handle customer complaints with a sense of urgency.

Some techniques are developed to improve sales.

Chapter 2

SALES SYSTEMS

It takes systems to be consistent and productive. The various sales activities from your sales systems must be intentionally set. The sales processes that they use in making a customer make a purchase. Those who do these things in sequence are running sales systems. Whether they know it or not. These activities are responsible for your sales success. Once these sales systems work to get you the results that you are looking for, continue to upgrade them and expand your business with these systems that work for you.

- Your sales targets.
- What you sell and the price that you sell them.
- The design of your shop.
- The uniform that you wear.

- How to recruit your sales team.
- What you train them with.
- How they are trained.
- How they approach customers.
- How they address customers.
- Their demeanor.
- The use of technology.
- Marketing campaigns.
- The use of social media.
- The use of phones.
- How to engage prospective buyers on the phone.
- How complaints are handled.
- How are they recorded and accounted for?
- Product visibility.
- Making sure moving products are always in stock.

All these are part of your sales systems. What you should know is that we call these steps designed to get you more sales as sales systems, and you have to build these intentionally. There must be tactics to convert your visibility to money, which is what sales systems do for you. These sales systems are handled with skills, so we must have a business culture that promotes continuous sales skills development.

So, build your own sales systems. Your sales goals require sales systems to consistently deliver the desired results. Success requires systems, and sales success requires the same systems. Don't take it for granted. Top businesses that excel in selling their products have strong sales systems in place. You don't have to be told to know this. While those who are not aware of these systems think something beyond human understanding is responsible for success, those who know are aware that wherever you see development, progress, and success, systems are responsible for the results.

- Set your sales goals and work toward them.
- Select and build a great sales team.
- Continue to train your team.

You cannot predict your sales until you have sales systems. Build your sales systems for your retail shop. Whatever you are selling, you have your own sales system. It takes discipline to build sales systems. It takes a lot of focus to have your sales systems in place. Many situations will push back but focus on having your sales systems in place. It makes productivity easier if you have your systems in place.

There must be tactics to convert your visibility to money

Chapter 3

SELLING IS CASH

Selling is cash, and in tough times, focus on sales. The time that the business is struggling is when the little money left should go into anything that will bring in sales. The business's finances struggle when sales are low, and we must push for more sales when things are difficult. So many business people focus so much on the aesthetics of the business. How the business is branded and how the office is organized, but little attention is given to what brings in the cash, mainly sales. This way of running a business is the reason many entrepreneurs have cash flow issues. They spend so much to keep the business's operations and pay little attention to the sales. Pay more attention to the activities that improve sales, and your business will start to do well. You can do a lot if your sales improve in your business. In the economy that we have in our country, you cannot take selling for granted. There is little investor money or bank support at a sustainable interest rate.

Look around you there are so many products that you can sell. You only have to get a space and put products needed in the locality. You can start selling in your area if you have been struggling with your finances. It does not have to be anything spectacular. Just find something to sell and your finances will start to change. Don't make it complicated. Just find something to sell. If you are employed and you are still out of shape with your finances, then find something to sell in your free time. Things will start to improve. Selling is cash; never forget that. If you don't have cash, you are not selling anything. Those who are selling have money.

Stop making excuses.

- You can find many reasons to justify your situation.
- You will change your situation once you start to sell.

- Use your phone to promote what you are selling.
- Tell people about what you are selling. Do it with joy.

Don't play with selling. You have completed your National Service and don't know what to do, so find something to sell. It does not matter the product. Make it in demand in your areas, and people can afford it. Don't waste much of your time writing a proposal for people to give you money.

Find something to sell. Don't wait for money so that you can start. You have a network. You know people. Talk to people. Go to town. Go to the village.

Find something to sell. You will change your life. That product that you start to sell can easily become a business. You can change the finances of your business by selling intentionally.

- Build training packs for yourself and your sales team.

• We are more into retail sales in Africa than direct sales.

• You don't need respect and opinions from people to make sales.

Chapter 4

SALES SKILLS

Selling is a skill that is developed over time. Those who are good in sales are those who intentionally groom their sales skills. They give the needed training and knowledge to themselves and their team. Much of what we sell in our country is in retail, so the intention should be to sell more in our retail settings. When you are selling in your shop, you don't necessarily need those who come to buy from you to beg you to sell to them; you don't need to lord it over them. You don't need your customers to respect you before you sell to them; you don't need to feel good or appreciated before you make your customers comfortable selling to them. Make good sales, and you will start to have confidence in yourself and your business.

People who doubt the viability of your business will start to change when you begin to see sales and improvement in sales. Customize your sales and sell with the culture in mind. Those who live and understand the culture are the majority of the population. Selling with the culture in mind will automatically increase your customer base. When customers say NO, it does not mean they don't want to buy they want a better reason to buy. Don't just accept No from customers; find ways to sell the product's value.

Make your customers comfortable and welcome. Make them feel happy about doing business with you. Instill that culture in your business, and you will not lack sales. Go the extra mile to make sales and ensure your customers have a great experience doing business with you.

- Sell with conviction.
- Sell with confidence.
- Sell with pride.

Products don't have to be perfect, but you can sell knowing that you are giving the best treatment to those who purchase your products. Those who have the best sales tactics are the ones making tremendous sales. We work, we make money, and we buy with the money we have. Many of our people don't buy with credit cards, so their judgment before they make a purchase can be a bit different from those who shop with borrowed money on their cards. Know the difference.

Whether you are on the phone or in person, sell with respect. Respect means a lot to our people, and so do relationships. Remember these two when you are selling to us.

Selling does not depend on the one buying; it depends on the skill level of the one selling, how they handle the sale process and the customer's emotions. If you don't know this, you will think that selling is out of your power. You can predict your sales because they depend on your sales skills and the quality of sales skills you have developed over time.

Take full responsibility for your sales performance, and you will see progress.

- Selling is a skill
- Serve your customers
- Make them comfortable
- Go the extra mile
- Convince them to buy
- Selling does not depend on the buyer
- Not the perfect product that sells
- It is who has strong sales systems
- Train your team
- Sell with the culture in mind
- We use cash to buy
- Handle aftersales professionally

Chapter 5

SELL ON VALUE

Sell on the value of the product you sell to the customer. If you don't know how to start any business, just start to sell something. Selling on value will mean that you and your sales team must have proper product knowledge of what you are selling. Customer must know that you know what you are talking about. What is the product made from, and what was the product made from? Focus on what the customer will get by parting with their money for the product or service. To do this, you must know the qualities of the product that you are selling. Learn every bit of its qualities and share with the customer as the point of purchase. The customer makes decisions based on the words that you are speaking and how well you speak them. Humans have emotions, and how well you appeal to these emotions goes a long way in determining customers' purchasing decisions.

- What are the positive aspects of the product that you are selling to the customer?

- What are the difficulties that the product will reduce for the customer?

- What pleasure will the product give to the customer?

People will keep coming back to you based on the value they gain from you and how you make them feel about themselves. How easy life becomes for them. Whenever you are selling, keep those in mind. Selling on value brings in more sales. This means that always keep in mind what the customer will get in exchange is his or her money and find a way to let the customer know what they are getting. If you are rendering service, let your customer feel welcome and respected. Let them know you are there to give the best service. As much as possible, don't let your customer feel like I will never come to this place again. It is a horrible service. Give the best of service and in many times is in customer feeling heard and attended to. Many people spend a lot of money to open a business but find no time to give the best service to their customers.

- Sell on value, and your business will thrive.
- Sell on value, and your customer will remember you
- Sell on value, and your customers will appreciate you.

...know the qualities of the product that you are selling.

Chapter 6

SALES AND MARKETING

Sell on the value of the product you sell to the customer. If you don't know how to start any business, start to sell something. Selling on value will mean that you and your sales team must have proper product knowledge of what you are selling. The customers must know that you know what you are talking about. What is the product made from? Focus on what the customer will get by parting with their money for the product or service. To do this, you must know the qualities of the product that you are selling. Learn every bit of its qualities and share with the customer at purchase. The customer makes decisions based on the words that you are speaking and how well you speak. Humans have emotions, and how well you appeal to these emotions goes a long way in determining customers' purchasing decisions.

- What are the positive aspects of the product you are selling to the customer?

- What are the difficulties that the product will reduce for the customer?

- What pleasure will the product give to the customer?

People will keep coming back to you based on the value they gain from you and how you make them feel about themselves. How easy life becomes for them. Whenever you are selling, keep those in mind. Selling on value brings in more sales. This means that always remember what the customer will get in exchange for his or her money and find a way to let the customer know what they are getting. If you are rendering service, let your customer feel welcome and respected. Let them know you are there to give the best service. As much as possible, don't let your customer feel never to come back. It is a horrible service. Give the best of service; often, it is in the customer's feeling heard and attended to. Many people spend a lot of money to open a business but find no time to give the best service to their customers.

- Sell on value, and your business will thrive.
- Sell on value, and your customer will remember you
- Sell on value, and your customers will appreciate you. ales and Marketing

Selling is money. Selling is cash. Marketing works on the prominent structure to make your service or product known. It involves a lot of the activities of the product. The adverts, the banners, the visibility, etc. After all is done, selling lets the customer part with their money for the product. Marketing is the framework that you work with. The campaign is marketing. In our business space, if you don't have a lot of money to spare, then focus on selling, focus on getting the cash. If you don't do the sales, you will struggle with money, and once the business starts to struggle with cash, you start to have challenges. Those who can quickly pick up their business are those who have a good cash flow from day one by mastering selling.

Don't just want your business name to be out without having the correspondent sales. After all the marketing, it costs money. Keep in mind that you must convert all your marketing tactics into sales. If you can do that, your business will start to see prospects. Your marketing activities must bring in cash, which will require good sales techniques from you and your team.

An entrepreneur with a strict budget must not just focus on marketing structures but on getting cash by selling the product or the services. Don't lose track. Keep the sales in mind all the time. Selling is cash.

- It is the campaign
- It is the structure
- It is what most people spend money on
- Don't overspend on this
- Convert to sales

Chapter 7

CUSTOMER SERVICE

It is tough to have a successful business without a strong sales advantage, and it is also challenging to have a strong sales advantage without very good customer service. It takes time to build a productive customer service culture; once it is built, it sticks with the business for a long time. How our customers feel when patronizing our service is pivotal to great customer service. It is about how people think about our product, service, and business. You have got to serve your customers with the best of service intentionally. People should bypass many similar companies offering what you do to come to you to do business with you. Respect your customer's sense of intelligence. Humans are social beings and emotional beings. Build a business customer culture that considers humans' social and emotional attachment.

Customer service is given in the culture, so don't forget to serve with the culture in mind. The way of the people is the culture. It is what they know. It is how they do things. It is what is comfortable for them. Serve with these in mind. Serve in the language they know, speak, and understand what they wear. What they eat. What they practise. The business will see growth when you mindfully give great customer service. The customers that come to you should keep returning and guarantee that you give them what they want with excellence. Don't only train yourself; train your team as well with the best of the service you want to give to your customers.

Customers come in different shapes and forms.
- Some are rich; some are poor.
- Some are educated and some are not.
- Some know about your business, some don't know you.
- Some are friendly, and some are learning to be friendly.

Plan to improve your customer service as the days go by. This is one area that many of our businesses have to know. It must be considered as one of the critical things in our culture that can promote quality customer service and inculcate it in our training and our customer service culture. Your customers deserve the best when they are yet to buy from you when buying, and after they have made the purchase.

The business will see growth when you mindfully give great customer service.

Chapter 8

SALES TARGETS

Having targets sets any one of us on the path to achievement faster. Targets concentrate our efforts for greater efforts. Develop your own sales targets on a daily, weekly, monthly, and yearly basis. If you don't have targets, then your sales success is left to chance. You win today; you struggle tomorrow. You win again, and then you lose. Those who don't have targets are more likely to give up on any little challenges. Those with targets work to achieve their goals. Have targets in terms of the numbers and what you want to sell for a specific time, not only in terms of products but also the money made from sales. If you are selling GHC 100,000 per month, you can say that I want to make two times that in the next month. That decision to meet that target will bring in more creativity and focus your energy to achieve your goals.

- Set targets and work towards them
- Set your targets as though you have already achieved them.
- Remind yourself constantly of your targets

You have to have goals and work towards those goals. It is very tough to achieve anything significant in life if you don't have something in mind that you want to achieve. Be someone with targets you are working towards, and your sales must have targets. Your sales targets largely depend on you and how you are determined to achieve them. Don't just wish that you will make those sales. You have to have daily, weekly, monthly, and yearly targets.

- Your sales targets will direct your sales.
- Your sales targets will focus your energy
- Your sales targets will make you not waste a lot of your energy

Never underestimate the impact of having sales targets on your money. Many people are intentional about their sales and how much they expect for a

particular period, which makes significant sales dif-
ferences. Keep on, no matter the challenges you meet
in meeting your sales targets. Challenges should not
prevent you from getting to your goals. Challenges
are part of the target process. They are not meant
to stop you. They are meant to help you build the
capacity to do more.

Create an environment where it is easy to meet your
targets. Have a circle of people working for you to
meet your targets. Surround yourself with things
that make you focus on your targets.

Chapter 9

SALES TRAINING

Training makes a lot of difference, and we are primarily made out of the training that we have had. Please don't give up on people until you have exposed them to the needed training. Humans can be trained to do well, which should be part of our national thinking and business practices. We all know how many of our people complain about our people's work ethics, yet they hardly make training part of the requirement for productivity - training tailored to develop the right mindset and skill set from the team. Selling is a skill that is developed when we are subjected to the training needed for the desired results. Regarding Africans, especially those of us in Ghana, what you need to train your sales team and yourself should be customized.

Many of the people you have employed in your shop or sales business are looking for what they call the opportunity to travel outside the Country.

Many do not link their growth in life to their work; they believe their religious and spiritual beliefs will make them do well. Others are looking for another chance to return to school and get a better job and salary. You must develop a sales force that can think and work to get the results you are looking for. This takes time, and without a proper cultural understanding of the people's behavior, you will continue to complain and feel frustrated.

You have to tell them about the products and services you offer and how they have to sell to the people. Don't just hope that they will work just because they have come to work; that is the mistake of many business owners. They expect so much from the people they have not systemically and continually trained.

What techniques do you use to recruit your sales team, and what things do you look out for? If you do these well, you have at least the basic requirements.

- Don't pick your sales team based on pity and sympathy
- Make sure there is some level of social skills and cultural awareness
- They should not be people who are moody and unfriendly
- They should have basic thinking abilities.

Test them on basic mathematical abilities. They must understand basic addition, subtraction, division, and multiplication. They should be ethical and not so much superstitious and over-religious. Their judgment must be based on facts, not their religious beliefs alone. If you want the best results from your team, you must always give the best training. You don't have to train them in English and what they call formal. Train them in the language that they understand and have control. Give examples from the environment that they live and help them to give the best of services based on the culture and not what you think is standard somewhere

Chapter 10

SALES TECHNIQUES

There are techniques you must be aware of and practice to get your sales to the best of the figures. You have to ensure the products you sell are visible to those who need the product or the service. It will be hard for them to procure products they don't know exist. Make the products visible. Doing that takes a lot of effort, but you must do it. Use any means necessary to put your products out there.

Visibility is key to selling. Your products should be very much accessible to your customers. It should not be difficult to assess your products, and products should also be easy to use. Remember, you are not making the product so much for you but for others to use. Some people are so much in love with their products that they don't have ears to listen to what their customers have to say. The next one is to ensure your customers feel needed and welcome to the shop. Bossing around your customers may not be such a nice idea. You want your customers to feel you are there to serve them and serve them well. You have no business if there is no customer for your products. Keep that in mind and the mind of your team. Build great relationships with your customers and make them feel important. For those in shops, we should not be on our phones when our customers are in the shop trying to make a purchase. Give maximum attention to your customers; after all, you are at the shop to sell and should sell. Don't let social media disturb the selling experience. Greet them on the phone or in the shop and talk respectfully and attentively. Your customer should feel special. Don't drop your sales because you are not paying attention to your customers. If I come to your shop and you are not paying attention, why should I come again? Once I have an option, I may not come there again. The experiences you give your customers will make them want to come to you to buy all the time because of how they feel when they do business with you.

Chapter 11

SALES TEAM

You will do great wonders with your sales if you have a great team; if a great team is built, there is no chance. It is developed. A team that is grateful for their work and who are positive and collaborative. A team that is not toxic to one another is a team that you can trust. Intentionally pull a team that is committed to becoming better on its own. Your business will not do well if the team is not ethical in their dealings. If you can get many team members to be people with strong life principles, especially when it comes to honesty and money, then you indeed have a great team. What is the point in having a great team that is stealing the sales that they make? That will put the business in trouble and eventually put you out of business.

Personal hygiene is taken seriously by the team, and the team's communication is constantly being improved. The team's bloodline is communication, so if the communication is not good, then there is no team fluency. If you have a team that is only interested in their salary and the money they have to make, they will not be committed to the vision of the business and will not sacrifice to make the needed sales.

Make sure you work on commission systems that bring the best out of your team, where their rewards are linked to their productivity. In that case, those who are lazy will not be happy to work with you. Build a sales culture where people are so glad to come to work and perform simultaneously. The team must know the value of time and should not come to work to waste time.

Teach your team how to work to get results. Team your team on how to sell and how to increase sales. Your team should know that they are the ones to bring in the sales, and the sales depend on them and no one else. A team trained to sell to customers well and handle customers' complaints without a fight with them or among themselves. Sometimes, you go to some shops, and you can easily see that the sales team does not have energy and is not there to sell to you. They have to come to work so that they can be paid. It takes a team to get the job done; you cannot work alone and build a team. Develop a team-driven sales culture where the team will do much of the work. That is when you have time to do other things as a business owner.

Chapter 12

PRODUCT KNOWLEDGE

The product is the reason the customer is connected to the business. The product is why the customer will part with his or her money. So, the knowledge that quickly gets the customer's attention is your knowledge about the product. We must sell the value of the product to the customer. The knowledge the team has about the product that we sell has a significant impact on the selling process. The team must know what the product is and where it is made from. The quality of the materials used to make the product, the good things about the products, and even the other side of the product that will have to do with the comfort and the safety of the customer. Product knowledge is what carries the value of the product to the customer.

There must be training routines for the team and yourself on the products your business sells, and it should not be a one-time show but a continuous process to keep the team updated on the products. Knowledge of how the product is used and how it is maintained. When to use the product and what to expect when the product is in use. How to maintain the product, and so on. Talk a lot about the value that the customer gains by buying the product. The team should not just provide good customer relationships and experience but must also give the proper knowledge about the product. The information we offer about the product to the customer affects their decision on the product and whether they will buy it. We make decisions with information and how the customer is comfortable about the product's value, the conviction that they are getting the correct value for their money when they make a purchase. Focus on selling based on product value by gaining the proper product knowledge. Sometimes, you can go to shops to ask for an item, and the salesperson there may not know what the product is or how it works. This sends the wrong message to your customers. It sends the message that your team is not trained and the team is not serious. Train them in the language they control and in the language your customer can easily understand. When new people join your team, let the old staff assist them until they are conversant with the product.

The information we offer about the product to the customer affects their decision

Chapter 13

OBJECTIONS

You have to know that when customers say no to buying a product, they often want to be convinced that they are making the right decision. Don't just say ok next time. Take responsibility for discovering the reason behind the no and discuss the value the customer gains by buying the product. You can go to some shops where the salesperson will take your number without trying to get you to purchase the item. I think it comes from their inability to handle objections from customers. Talk about the product's benefits and talk with respect and confidence.

Remember, no from a customer does not mean they don't have money or they don't want to buy; they want better reasons to make a purchase, and that is the point you must pull out your sales skills. Learn not to let nos stop you from selling. See the nos as a state that you must handle with composure to equip the customer with better information to buy from you. It is a bit uncomfortable to hear no from a customer. Part of the selling process is learning not to be surprised by objections from your prospects. Many people cannot take no, which is why they are uncomfortable with selling the products or services. They take things so personally, but it should not be so. Even though it is hard, just know that is part of the process, and I am sure with training and time, you will become a little bit more skilled in handling the nos from customers. Talk about product benefits, stay pleasant, and stay confident. Assure your clients that they are getting value for money. Even if they don't make a purchase, you should be proud of yourself that you have made some effort. Don't just lay back and be distracted by the fear of customers telling you they are not interested or they are not making a purchase. You have to be strong to make sales. Some days can be that good, and some days can be dragging. Learn to handle the objects, and your sales will increase. Selling is a process, and selling is about people. People have emotions, and people make choices. Help with the right tools to make the decisions that will increase your sales.

- Know how to handle the Nos from your customers
- It is not that they don't want to buy
- They don't want to be cheated
- Don't just say ok
- Talk about the product and the benefit
- The customer is using your words to make decisions
- Take note of the emotions of your customers and the words you use
- Don't sell with your pocket in mind
- You may not be able to afford some of the products in the shop for yourself, but that should not mean anyone your age cannot afford them.

Chapter 14

COMPLAINTS AND AFTER SALES

You must have protocols to handle the complaints that come from your customers after they have made a purchase. You should hold this stage with enthusiasm, especially in our country. People should not feel that your business does not care after buying from you and that something they did not expect to happen needs to be sorted out. The complaints from your customers are part of the sales process. The sales process does not end after taking money. Suppose there are issues after you make sales; your customer should be confident that you will solve their problems as quickly as possible and as needed. Don't build a business culture that does not listen to customers' complaints. If you handle this well, your business will be above and beyond those that don't take customers' complaints seriously. You must ensure your customers' concerns are addressed to their satisfaction. There will be those who like to take advantage but are usually not the majority, so find a way to bear with them.

Build simple processes that handle complaints and make sure that there is a way some of these complaints get to you as the leader of the business. There should be a way for the complaints to be documented with the customer's time, date, and contact number for the problem. There should be ways to keep the customer updated on how the complaint is being addressed. This makes things a bit easier. Assign complaints to team members who are not forgetful and who take their work seriously. Try to make complaints from your customers personally so that you give them the attention they need to solve them. Your number should not be far from your team and your customers. Many challenges can easily be rectified if these problems find ways to get to your notice on time. Don't be so big that customers' issues don't get to you. You have a business because your customers do business or buy from you. Their concerns should be your priority. This is one of the best ways to keep many of your customers. When they know that you are there to solve their problems. Customer retention has much to do with handling complaints if your customers feel listened to, they will always want to come back.

Chapter 15

SOCIAL MEDIA

In the times that we live in, many of us have access to social media. It is very cheap technology, and it is the easiest way to promote our products and services. Many people build business and personal brands quickly and easily because of social media. Young men and women are selling all kinds of products through social media. Please don't stay out and say it is not happening. From YouTube to X, TikTok, WhatsApp to Facebook, and Instagram to Snapchat. Use these tools to promote your products and to make more sales. Use audio, pictures, and videos to promote your products and to make sales. Any phone with a good camera can do wonders. The internet and social media have brought a lot of opportunities to many people who otherwise could not have these opportunities. In Ghana, many of our young people sell volumes of products on their Facebook accounts or TikTok. Some are even selling with their WhatsApp status. Once you can access people, you can promote your products and make sales. There are YouTube channels that have more followers than media houses, and they can promote product sales more than some of the major media houses. When you start, it can drag a bit, but with consistency and determination, you can build a following, and once you have a good following, you can have a community that can help you promote your products and make your sales. A lot has changed with the coming of social media, and that phone in your hand is a sales tool; make good use of it. Don't let others convince you that you are posting too much. It is your phone, so keep posting until you have the audience that you are looking for. Social media also serve as avenues to improve your communication, marketing, and sales skills. By constantly practising you become better, not only in your product promotion but in your sales skills. Social media gives visibility as well, with very little setup and no cost. Promote your products and skills with social media. Businesses have come out of social media accounts because people were serious about it.

I know people who have created groups using social media, and those groups sell all kinds of products and form all types of business alliances. That is the power of social media. Study social media marketing and do it well.

Chapter 16

SELL WITH THE CULTURE

Sell with the culture in mind. Once you understand the culture of the people, you can sell to them. The people are socialized in their culture. Their way of doing things. Their way of life. Their language, their beliefs, and their outlook on life. If you are going to sell to any people, you don't try to sell to them outside that which they are comfortable and familiar with. You can easily struggle with your sales when you try to sell.

Trying to sell without the culture in mind is like trying to sell winter clothes to those of us in Ghana. The weather does not support that. Remember, you are selling products that the people need at a price point that they can afford and with customer service that they see as respected and appreciated.

They must feel welcome and served well. Don't just try to superimpose your way of selling from another culture to them at all costs. Even if you want to introduce any new thing, it should be done with the culture in mind, and it should be done gradually and with cultural sensitivity. That is the way to win.

- Don't forget where the people come from.
- Don't forget the belief system of those that you are selling to.

When you introduce any new techniques or training, don't forget the culture of the community to which you are selling. Don't just tell us it is the international standard. It is standard so long as those using it are comfortable and safe. Study other ways of improving things but improve with the culture in mind. Grow with culture in mind. Innovate with the culture in mind. Learn to improve the way things are done. In our culture, we hold in high esteem, respect, peace, and acceptance. No matter what you bring to us, if you don't come with these, it will not be sustainable. The culture is communal, and the people are very sociable. Even if you are introducing technology, study how people do their things at a certain point in time, and it will help the situation. The sales will improve when you keep the culture in mind.

- Sell what the culture wants.
- Sell what the culture can easily use.
- Sell what the culture can afford.
- Sell what is in demand in the culture. Sell what the culture values

Chapter 17

SALES ETHICS

Don't take the intelligence of your customers for granted. Don't just sell anything to them for profit. You will eventually lose out. Keep your word and let your business be known as a business that can be trusted. Let your word be your bond to your customers. Be honest in your dealings. Don't sell things that you know are not what you promised. The best way to stay on the journey for a long time is to stay honest. When you are ethical and you serve your customers well you have long-term business and it is one of the best ways to grow your sales and your business. Selling is cash as they say and with cash coming to your business, you have the opportunity to grow.

You will make some mistakes along the line but make it your mantra to be ethical in your sales and you will not have anything to hide. Don't find excuses to be dishonest; if you want to be that, you can find many reasons to do that. Keep your promise to your customers and they will find many ways to be loyal to you. Faking things will work back against you. You don't have to be rich quickly through dubious means. Stick with your morals. Stick with your value. Have convictions. Develop strong values and your business will go a long way. There will be tempting situations and people will always try to convince you to go against what you have decided not to do when it comes to that point. Refer to your values and you will be fine. In difficult moments still stay with your values. When nobody will find out let your conscience be your guide. This kind of lifestyle is the one that will protect you from falling or from disaster. When it even happens that you fall you will get back up because you stand for the right thing. Sell with ethics and you will have business all the time.

- Many are destroyed because of greed.
- Many are destroyed because they want to cut corners.
- Many are destroyed because they were dishonest.
- Protect your dignity
- Sell with character

Train your team with your sales ethics. Show your customer respect and make sure your sales team does the same

Chapter 18

MAKE IT A GREAT EXPERIENCE

Selling is an experience, and so make it an excellent experience for those who come to buy from you. They hardly forget any bad experiences they go through with you, and they remember any good experiences they go through by buying from you. Train your team to make sure that customer experience is also their priority in the sales process. Humans have emotions, and they make decisions based on how they feel wanted and respected. Respect is currency, and you can get into the hearts of many people if they feel respected, listened to, or welcomed. Your sales team should pay attention to the experience they give to customers because that is a large part of the very things they remember after they make a purchase. '

Please don't give a bad attitude to your customers, and don't make them feel like they are begging you to buy from you. It is often an honor on your part to have a business that is providing the service that is needed.

You should have a sales culture that is fully aware of the experience that they are giving to customers. If they do good work, they should know, and if they don't do well too, they should be as aware. They should not be oblivious to what customer pick from the business by their encounter with the business. Great customer service cannot be devoid of great customer experience. Great customer experience, great sales. You put your business on a different level when you are determined to give a great customer experience. It takes time to build a sales culture so that customers don't get shocked by the quality of the services that you give them.

Develop mechanisms to always improve your sales knowledge and skills and those of your team. Remember, until the money is taken, the selling is not completed. Serve your customers with respect, and those who know this in our culture are able to grow their business well. Make your customers feel comfortable and go the extra mile to make your customers experience the best of service.

AFTERWORD

Building a successful business and even wealth requires selling, and our ability to sell our ideas, products, and services is so important. It does not matter what solutions or products we have; we must have ways to sell what we have, and until we sell, the process is not completed. Many of us master every technical skill except selling, and yet that is the skill that brings in the money. The way money comes in is by selling; the other activities are taking money from you and your business, and selling is what is bringing money. This is the reason that we must sell. Many of us don't have loans, and others invest their money. We must learn to sell our business idea and what the business does to others.

We must always keep our environment in mind, the culture we sell in, and the culture we sell to. We cannot do much until we understand the culture that we operate in. Optimize technology in our selling process, and we must know how to develop our selling skills and develop our sales team. Even if you don't know what business to get into, find a product that you can sell that is in high demand, and you can quickly start to get a business.

Selling does not depend on the buyer; it depends on how you sell. You don't have to have a perfect product to sell; you must know how to sell what you have. The tactics that have helped you sell should be structured, and that becomes your own sales systems that are unique to your business, which you can use to train your team. Handle your aftersales professionally and learn to give great service on the phone as well.

Made in the USA
Las Vegas, NV
21 June 2025